MANDRAGOLA

The Library of Liberal Arts
OSKAR PIEST, FOUNDER

MANDRAGOLA

NICCOLÒ MACHIAVELLI

Translated by
ANNE AND HENRY PAOLUCCI
with an introduction by
HENRY PAOLUCCI

· ·

The Library of Liberal Arts

THE BOBBS-MERRILL COMPANY, INC.
PUBLISHERS · INDIANAPOLIS · NEW YORK

Niccolò Machiavelli: 1469-1527

COPYRIGHT ©, 1957

THE LIBERAL ARTS PRESS, INC.
A DIVISION OF THE BOBBS-MERRILL COMPANY, INC

All Rights Reserved
Printed in the United States of America
Library of Congress Catalog Card Number: 57-14629
ISBN 0-672-60231-8 (pbk)
Ninth Printing

CONTENTS

. . . .

TRANSLATOR'S INTRODUCTION

Machiavelli's *Mandragola,* for centuries half-hidden from view in the shadow of *The Prince,* has only lately begun to receive adequate recognition as what it unquestionably is: the unrivaled masterpiece of the Italian comic theater. Carlo Goldoni, the eighteenth-century author traditionally honored as Italy's foremost comic playwright, will, no doubt, because of the mere quantity of good work he produced, continue to be so honored; nevertheless, the best Italian critics today are inclined to uphold the judgment of T. B. Macaulay that the *Mandragola* "is superior to the best of Goldoni and inferior only to the best of Molière." [1] They agree that no one work of Goldoni rises to the level of dramatic perfection of the *Mandragola.* They recognize also that precisely where Goldoni's art seems weakest as compared with Molière's—in intellectual fiber and depth of characterization—Machiavelli's art is exceptionally strong; and some critics press the advantage even further, noting that Machiavelli displays technical mastery also in the one phase of dramatic art wherein Molière himself was admittedly weak, namely, in the architectural design of the action, in the unraveling of the plot, which, as Voltaire observed, is often brought on in Molière with too little preparation and in an improbable manner. Voltaire, incidentally, is said to have asserted that the *Mandragola* was "worth more than all the comedies of Aristophanes." [2] One might more justly assert, rather, that had Machiavelli been willing to divert himself with writing a few more plays of comparable merit, and had he not written *The Prince* and the *Discourses,* he would long

[1] Thomas Babington Macaulay, "Machiavelli," in *Macaulay, Prose and Poetry,* selected by G. M. Young (Cambridge, Mass., 1952), p. 252. The essay was originally printed in the *Edinburgh Review,* March, 1827.

[2] See preface by I. D. Levine in Niccolò Machiavelli, *Mandragola,* tr. Stark Young (New York, 1927), pp. 8-9.

ago have been acclaimed a master of comedy to be ranked as the equal of Aristophanes and Molière.

Two other comedies, both typical products of the Renaissance theater, have come to us from the pen of Machiavelli: *Andria,* translated from Terence, and *Clizia,* an imitation of Plautus. But in the *Mandragola,* written sometime between 1512 and 1520, Machiavelli rose above the Renaissance ideal, abandoning translation and imitation for pure invention. Spectators at its earliest performances (one of the first took place in the year 1520 in the presence of Pope Leo X) judged the play to be something distinctly new—and modern literary scholars generally have concurred in that judgment.

The theme of the play, sexual seduction, is, of course, not new. A love-sick young man enlists the aid of servants, friends, and rogues that he may gratify an inordinate desire to possess the beautiful wife of an old "doctor"; obstacles are encountered; plans to overcome them are devised and revised; at last, after a series of humorous turns, the desired end is attained. All this belongs to comic tradition. Machiavelli, however, introduces an element that makes a fundamental difference. He represents the beautiful wife as an evidently virtuous woman who would not under any circumstances invite amorous advances and who has not the least intention of betraying her husband. Remarking the novelty of this representation of the wife, Professor D. C. Stuart, in his *Development of Dramatic Art,* observes that as a consequence "scenes and situations unknown in Latin comedy are introduced." [3] But this novel characterization is by no means accidental. It is, itself, a consequence of Machiavelli's wholly original conception of the basic action of the play. With the genius of purest comedy evidently guiding him, he boldly manipulates the commonplace amorous intrigue which is his theme as if it were a problem in international diplomacy. From the outset, the young hero of the play seems as ardently concerned to secure emotional health

[3] Donald Clive Stuart, *Development of Dramatic Art* (New York and London, 1928), p. 286.

for himself as some fiery statesman might well be to secure the *salus republica*. He represents himself as caught in a situation of clear and present danger; he must attain his end or be destroyed. And with very life at issue, the voice of reason itself, he tells us, dictates that he must be willing to do whatever necessity indicates to secure victory and, with victory, the enjoyment of that hallowed peace and happiness which is the goal of all human endeavor.

In pursuit of such happiness the young hero enters, conditionally, upon an alliance with a known ruffian who performs his services with the aplomb of an experienced official of the diplomatic corps. The ruffian warns against shortsightedness, against unnecessary violence, against the allurements of easy but merely temporary success; and he advises a definition of policy such that everyone involved may anticipate from its successful execution some real or apparent benefit. The task, thereafter, is merely to negotiate with all parties, pointing out to each the nature of the advantage to be derived, beginning with those whose advantage is most obvious (even if only apparent) and, with their support, proceeding to the persuasion of the one person who, seemingly at least, stands to lose something precious in the transaction. Bluntly stated, the immediate object is to enlist the aid of husband, mother, and father confessor in persuading a virtuous wife that she shall have performed a faithful act of conjugal obedience while admitting an utter stranger to the enjoyments of her bed. Such is the immediate object; the ultimate object is to effect in the wife a fundamental "transvaluation of values."

The attainment of these two objects involves the chief personages of the play in a series of actions which prompts Professor Stuart to remark: "Of the cynical immorality of these situations the less said the better; but nevertheless these scenes strike a note never heard even in Plautus. They give an opportunity for dramatic progression." [4] And even the great Francesco de Sanctis, who otherwise judges the *Mandragola* very severely on moral grounds, is constrained to acknowledge that in

4 *Ibid.*

the closing scenes Machiavelli rises to a display of "comic
power and originality matched by little in the ancient or
modern theater." [5]

The chief personages of the play—the Prologue informs us
—are four: a low-designing lover, a leech or ruffian who is "deceit's own child," an absurdly pompous old "doctor," and a
monk who has lived ill. We have already considered briefly
the characterizations of the young lover and his ruffian adviser.
The old "doctor" is, of course, the butt of the farcical intrigue.
A scrawny old pigeon of a man, he struts and cackles among
women and servants, bows and scrapes before his betters, and
scurries out of sight at the mere suggestion of real danger. He
is vulgar, stupid, impotent, shameless; but Machiavelli mas-
terfully elevates him to the level of high comedy by arming
him with the proverbial wisdom of the common people. His
speech is a *vade mecum* of popular sagacity. His every decision, his every deed has the sanction of some traditional Florentine proverb, so that the old fool has the satisfaction of thinking himself a veritable fox as he leads himself by the nose
whither others want him to go.

The fourth chief personage, the monk who has lived ill,
makes his appearance very late in the play. The Prologue
warns us that we may miss him if we hurry away too soon. And
yet he is unmistakably the most important personality, so profoundly complex that there have been almost as many diverse
interpretations of his character and of the significance of his
part in the play as there have been critics. In the judgment of
some he is a cheap hypocrite, a deceitful casuist and simoniac
trading for a pittance the spiritual goods entrusted to his care,
a lecherous corrupter of womanhood, of family, of society.
For others he is a delightfully Boccaccesque personality, by
some quirk of fate thrust into a monkish order, conducting
himself as well as one can under the circumstances and con-
senting, when he cannot graciously do otherwise, to spice our

[5] Francesco de Sanctis, *Storia della letteratura italiana* (Milano, 1928),
II, 89.

enjoyment of the venereal suggestiveness of the play with a touch of clerical wit. Still other critics have seen in him a frank spokesman for Machiavelli's own profoundest sentiments regarding the nature of man and the motives underlying the normal conduct of human affairs.

He is, indeed, as some of the best critics have suggested, exactly the same sort of enigmatic personality that Machiavelli's prince is. The latter, too, has been variously appraised, being most frequently denounced as the embodiment of absolute immorality, yet almost as often admired for his unwavering pragmatism, and sometimes even quite earnestly acclaimed as the only conceivable instrument of temporal salvation for a politically depressed people. Each of these diverse interpretations, of the monk as of the prince, contains a large measure of truth; each is the result of appraising a singularly rich personality from a different point of view. The fact that Machiavelli, with the instinct of a dramatist, declines to impose upon his readers any single point of view is, perhaps, a defect in *The Prince,* for it renders equivocal the meaning of a work that may have been intended to be clear and unambiguous. But it is no defect in the *Mandragola* and, indeed, no defect in *The Prince* either, if the latter be judged from a purely literary standpoint. So judged *The Prince* becomes a grand tragedy— a play, rather than a treatise, offering a tragic view of the same world of which the *Mandragola* is the comedy.

Machiavelli, it would seem, was incapable of delineating an unequivocal representation of the world underlying his literary masterpieces. At any rate, one looks in vain through the entire corpus of his writings for such a picture. Here and there, especially in the *Discourses,* in the lesser tracts, and in the *Florentine Histories,* profoundly suggestive indications are given, but always in a fragmentary, and frequently in a self-contradictory or, rather, paradoxical manner. Yet the indications are sufficient to enable a serious student of political philosophy to recognize their compatibility with that grand conception of ethics and politics, and of the interrelation of the two in history, which had its foundation in Aristotle and which has received its most systematic exposition, from a secular point of view, in the *Philosophy of Law* of Hegel. Its equivalent in traditional Christianity is to be found in St. Augustine's elaborate conception of the *civitas terrena.*

The world of the *Mandragola* and of *The Prince* is a world of men, women, and children all earnestly pursuing peace and happiness, yet unfortunately pursuing these wonderful ends in such a way that the satisfaction of one person often, if not always, involves the frustration of another. Conflicts of interest inevitably arise—between the crying infant and its mother, between children, youths, adults, families, clans; and in these conflicts either both parties are frustrated or one party emerges as victor and the other as vanquished. No doubt there have always been some human beings who would rather die than submit to the will of another, but these have, in fact, been such rarities that all peoples, at all times, have looked upon them with wonderment. The majority of human beings easily learn to accommodate themselves in defeat, submitting their wills, gradually, as well as their bodies to the guidance of their conquerors. Thus emerges that "consent of the governed," that common will, which transforms the relation of victor and vanquished into that of ruler and ruled. The institution of law and education is then possible, the latter implementing the former by training youths, from the earliest possible moment, to conduct themselves habitually in accordance with the common will. The product of the common will is the commonwealth, or *res publica.*

A people with a *res publica* are able to enjoy much peace and happiness among themselves—provided they can secure their commonwealth against the inevitable aggressions of their richer and poorer neighbors. If they can, they will no doubt continue to prosper, augmenting their commonwealth, insuring domestic tranquillity, and providing for the common defense first by merely thrusting back aggressors who invade their peaceful land, later, with more prudence, going forth to meet and stop aggressors before they actually invade, and finally, with maximum prudence, streaming outward themselves in full force to make the world utterly and forever safe, so that they who have proved most willing to fight for freedom may thereafter live comfortably in the peaceful pursuit of happiness.

So, according to the basic pattern glimpsed by Machiavelli, runs the course of the world's pursuit of happiness. Aristotle, in his *Politics,* concentrated his attention on the phase of this process which culminates in the establishment of a republic with sufficient means to facilitate among its free citizens the pursuit of knowledge and happiness. The Roman political and juridical thinkers concentrated on the problem of establishing the habits of peace throughout the world, putting an end to the aggressions of haughty people and helping backward areas to help themselves. St. Augustine, called upon to explain the sack of Rome in 410, chose to assess the colossal misery involved in the whole process, especially in its culminating stage—the establishing of an enforceable world peace.

In *The Prince* Machiavelli restricted himself to an analysis of the problem of releasing a vanquished people from the bondage of factional disunity imposed upon them by powerful neighbors. This is perhaps the ugliest phase of the process, especially from the point of view of the citizens of nations that have long ago solved the problem in question, and whose statesmen are masters of the high art of preventing other peoples from doing so. But in whatever phase men and societies may find themselves, the fundamental human nature, the underlying natural impulses, Machiavelli insists, remain the same. His view of human nature, pessimistic as it may seem, accords exactly with that of Aristotle, who observed that, apart from the restraints of politically constituted society, men are apt to behave toward one another worse than the most savage beasts; and it accords also with the traditional doctrine of Christianity on human nature, especially as articulated by St. Augustine. One should not forget, however, that in St. Augustine's view nature is not the sole force operating in human history. According to the great African bishop, Divine Grace also operates, sustaining, in the midst of the *civitas terrena,* a pilgrim portion of the City of God.

Of Divine Grace operating in the world, Machiavelli, need-less to say, saw nothing. From a Christian point of view, there-fore, one may say that his unpleasant doctrine is not the whole story. But, as T. S. Eliot has very emphatically observed in his short essay on the subject, from no other point of view can one fairly make this restriction.[6] Against modern readers who find themselves revolted by the immorality of the world of *The Prince* and the *Mandragola* and who, on that account, repudi-ate Machiavelli's representation of human nature as unrealis-tic or perhaps true only for Italians of his own time, T. S. El-iot has written significantly: "Machiavelli was no fanatic; he merely observed the truth about humanity without the addi-tion of superhuman Grace." His view, Eliot continues, "is therefore tolerable only to persons who have also a definite religious belief; to the effort of the last three centuries to sup-ply religious belief by belief in Humanity the creed of Machia-velli is insupportable." All that the author of *The Prince* and of the *Mandragola* failed to see about human nature, Eliot concludes, is "the myth of human goodness which for liberal thought replaces the belief in Divine Grace."

With the foregoing representation of the historical pattern of the earthly pursuit of happiness to serve as a background, it is perhaps easier to see why, judged from a purely literary standpoint, *The Prince* is indeed a tragedy and the *Man-dragola* a comedy. *The Prince* represents a desperate, utterly frustrate attempt to salvage some genuine happiness out of a wretched national situation; the *Mandragola,* on the other hand, represents a mere prank whereby an audience is in-vited, for its recreation, to observe how, even in the tragic land of *The Prince,* some small measure of delight may be secured by deception worked so cunningly and with so little violence as to inflict as little pain as possible upon those

---

[6] T. S. Eliot, "Niccolo Machiavelli," in *For Lancelot Andrews* (Garden City, N. Y., 1929), pp. 62-63.

who are being deceived. The spectacle of this cunningly worked deception may be enjoyed, on a thoughtless level, simply for its own sake. But appreciation of the element of greatness in the play requires that a picture of the tragic world of *The Prince* be ever kept at least faintly in mind. And Machiavelli is able to force upon his audience repeated reminders of the presence of that world primarily through his characterization of the monk, Fra Timoteo, to whom he has given that "inexplicable touch of infinity"—as A. C. Bradley calls it—which is the mark of true greatness in dramatic creation.

HENRY PAOLUCCI

NOTE ON THE TEXT

The present translation of the *Mandragola* is based primarily upon the Italian text included in G. Mazzoni and M. Casella (eds.), *Tutte le opere di Niccolò Machiavelli* (Florence, 1929).

A. P.

MANDRAGOLA

CHARACTERS

CALLIMACO, a young man
SIRO, his servant
MESSER NICIA, a "learned" doctor
LIGURIO, a local knave
SOSTRATA, mother-in-law of Messer Nicia
FRIAR TIMOTEO
A WOMAN
LUCREZIA, wife of Messer Nicia

SCENE

A public square in Florence

PROLOGUE

Good humored audience!
God grant you heaven's joys!
For your good humor seems to wish us well.
And now, if it please you to make no noise,
We have a good story we'd like to tell.
It happened in this town, the facts are true;
Here is the scene prepared for you.
Watch now, for the curtains are about to draw:
See beautiful Florence, that's your own home;
Perhaps we'll say it's Pisa next, or Rome.
(Don't laugh too hard, or you'll loosen your jaw.)

That doorway on my right
Is the house of a doctor of law
Who read Boethius and learned it all.
That street, the dingiest you ever saw.
Back there, is Lovers' Lane, where those who fall
Must give up hope that they can ever rise.
And next, you'll see with your own eyes
(If you don't leave before we start the play),
What sort of abbot lives in town;
You'll see him in his friar's gown,
Coming out of the church across the way.

Callimaco Guadagni,
A young man who has just returned
From Paris, lives on my left, at that door.
His fine dress and his charming ways have earned
For him the honors of first place before
All other dandies in society.
A lady of propriety
Was passionately loved by this young swain,

And tricked by him, as you shall see.
I wish that you might someday be
Tricked just as she was, with as little pain.

The tale is called Mandragola;
The reason for it you will see,
If I guess rightly, as the play unfolds.
The author is no great celebrity;
Yet, if he cannot make you laugh, he holds
Himself prepared to treat the house to wine.
A young lover of low design,
A monk who hasn't followed virtue's way,
A doctor easily beguiled,
A leech who is deceit's own child—
They'll entertain you in this evening's play.

And if the theme we offer,
Being so light, does not befit
A man who wishes to seem grave and wise,
Forgive him on this ground: he tries his wit
With trifles, hoping thus to minimize
The ordeal of a life full of concern;
And he has nowhere else to turn.
The world's indifference alone restrains
Him from attempting to display
His talents in a better way,
Since no reward is offered for his pains.

The reward to expect
Is that people will stand about
And grin, maligning what they hear or see.
And that suffices to explain, no doubt,
The total absence, in our century,
Of virtues cherished in the good old days;
For no one, when he finds no praise
Is given, will consume himself in toil,
Or take on endless cares, to bring

Into the world some precious thing
That fogs may cover up or winds may spoil.

And yet if anyone
Should think that he can push, or scare,
Or shake our author, by maligning him,
I must advise and warn him to beware
That our author can malign and trim
As well as he; that it was his first art;
Nor can you find in any part
Of this peninsula that rings with "si,"
A man he condescends to prize,
Though he may serve someone who buys
A more expensive suit of clothes than he.

But let anyone malign
If it pleases him; we must start
To tell our tale before the night is done.
The words you'll hear you mustn't take to heart;
And should you see some half-dead creature run
Across our stage, ignore him, let him go.
But look—here comes Callimaco
With Siro, his man; they will tell you where
The plot has led thus far. Now pay
Close attention to what they say,
For we propose to end our prologue here.

ACT I

SCENE 1

Callimaco, Siro.

CALLIMACO: Siro, hold on a minute. I want to see you.

SIRO: At your service.

CALLIMACO: You must have been puzzled by my sudden departure from Paris, and you're probably still puzzled now because I've already been here a whole month, doing nothing.

SIRO: That's true.

CALLIMACO: What I'm going to tell you now I haven't told you before, not because I don't trust you, but because I have always thought that when a person doesn't want certain things to be known, he mustn't mention them at all, unless he has to. Now, however, when it seems that I'm going to need your help, I want to tell you the whole story.

SIRO: I'm your servant: servants must never question their masters, or be curious about anything that concerns them; but when the masters themselves mention something, they must be willing to obey faithfully, as I have always done and am ready to do now.

CALLIMACO: Yes, I know. Perhaps you have already heard me explain a thousand times (but it won't hurt you to hear it a thousand and one) how it happened that, when I was ten, after my mother and father had died, my guardians sent me to Paris where I have been for the past twenty years. At the end of ten years, after the wars caused by King Charles' march through Italy had begun and were devastating that country, I decided to settle down in Paris, never to return to my native land, being convinced that I would find it safer to live there than here.

7

SIRO: That's right.

CALLIMACO: After arranging for the sale of all my property here, except the house, I established residence there, where I remained another ten years very contentedly—

SIRO: I know all that.

CALLIMACO:—with part of my time given to study, another part to entertainment, and the rest to business; and I managed to pursue these various interests in such a way that one never interfered with the others. That enabled me, as you know, to live quite peacefully, helping everyone and taking care to offend no one; so that it seemed to me that I was well liked by tradesmen, nobles, strangers, townspeople, the rich, the poor. . . .

SIRO: That's the very truth.

CALLIMACO: But since it seemed to Fortune that I was having too good a time, she saw to it that a certain Cammillo Calfucci should come to Paris.

SIRO: I'm beginning to see what's the matter with you.

CALLIMACO: He, like the other Florentines, often came to dinner at my house; and in the course of conversation one day we fell to arguing whether women were more beautiful in Italy or in France. Of course, I couldn't speak for the women of Italy, for I had left there when I was very young; so another Florentine who was present took the French side and Cammillo the Italian. And after many arguments back and forth, Cammillo, somewhat irritated, said that even if all Italian women were monsters, a certain relative of his could win back their lost prestige.

SIRO: Now I know what you're driving at!

CALLIMACO: And he named Donna Lucrezia, wife of Messer Nicia Calfucci, praising her so highly for her beauty and charm that he left us all gaping; and in me he aroused such a longing to see her that I threw everything else aside, forgot about war or peace in Italy, and started out to come here. And I found, when I got here, that what had been said in praise of Donna Lucrezia fell far short of the truth—something that happens very rarely; and now I'm steaming with such a burning desire to be with her that I can't find any relief.

SIRO: If you had told me about this in Paris, I would have known what to recommend, but now I don't quite know what I can say to you.

CALLIMACO: I haven't been telling you this to get your advice, but to unburden myself a little, and to make sure you'll be prepared to help me when the time comes.

SIRO: I'm already completely prepared; but what are your chances in this?

CALLIMACO: Unfortunately, none, or almost none. You see, what fights me off, first of all, is her completely honest nature, which is totally aloof from all the temptations of love; the fact that she has a husband who is very rich and lets himself be governed by her in all things, who may not be so young yet isn't quite as old as he looks; and also the fact that she doesn't have relatives or neighbors with whom she might spend an evening, or pass a holiday, or go to some other kind of entertainment young women usually enjoy. I don't know of any venal persons who frequent her house, and there isn't a girl about her, or servant, who isn't afraid of her; so there's no chance of getting anywhere by bribery.

SIRO: Then what do you think you'll be able to do?

CALLIMACO: Nothing's ever so completely a lost cause that there can't be some way to hope for it, even if it's only weak and empty; the passion and desire a person has to get what he wants keeps it from seeming so.

SIRO: In short then, what is it that makes you hope?

CALLIMACO: Two things. One is the utter simplicity of Messer Nicia, for, although he has a doctor's degree, he's the silliest and stupidest man in all Florence. The other is the longing they both have for children; for she's been married six years already without having had any, and, since they're very rich, their longing now makes them almost desperate. There is also a third thing: her mother used to like good times, but she's so rich now that I don't see how I can make use of it.

SIRO: But have you tried to do anything?

CALLIMACO: Yes I have, but it doesn't amount to much.

SIRO: What?

CALLIMACO: You know Ligurio, who always comes to eat at my house. He used to be a matchmaker in the old days, before he began grubbing dinners and suppers; anyway, because he's a likable fellow, Messer Nicia is friendly with him, and of course Ligurio plays along. Nicia doesn't invite him in to eat, but he does lend him money from time to time. I have made friends with him, and I've told him about this love of mine; he has promised to help me by hook or by crook.

SIRO: Don't be taken in by him: these grubbers are not the kind of people you can trust.

CALLIMACO: That's true; still, when there's an advantage in it for someone, and you point it out, I think you can count on him to do what he says. I've promised to give him a nice sum of money when and if he succeeds; if he doesn't succeed, he'll get a dinner and supper out of it, which I wouldn't care to eat alone anyway.

SIRO: What has he promised to do so far?

CALLIMACO: He has promised to persuade Messer Nicia that he ought to take his wife to the baths this May.

SIRO: What's that to you?

CALLIMACO: What's that to me? The baths might work a complete change of nature in her, for in places like that it's just one big holiday all the time; I'd go there, and I'd provide as many such pleasures as I could, not holding back at any expense, and I'd become friends with her and her husband. Who knows? One thing leads to another and only time can tell.

SIRO: That doesn't sound like a bad idea.

CALLIMACO: Ligurio left me this morning saying he would talk with Messer Nicia about this and would let me know what happens.

SIRO: There they are now, both of them.

CALLIMACO: I'm going to keep out of sight here so I can catch Ligurio and speak to him as soon as he leaves the doctor. Meanwhile, you get back into the house and tend to your work; if I want you for anything I'll let you know.

SIRO: I'm going.

SCENE 2

Messer Nicia, Ligurio.

MESSER NICIA: I don't doubt your suggestion is good, and I spoke to my wife about it last night. She said she'd give me the answer today; but to tell you the truth, I'll have to drag myself to go.

LIGURIO: Why?

MESSER NICIA: Why? Because I don't like to get tagged off base. Besides, to move wife, servants, and everything—it just doesn't square with me. And then, I talked to a lot of physicians last night: one says I should go to San Filipo, another to the Porretta, another to the Villa—they looked like a bunch of quacks to me. To tell you the truth, these doctors of medicine don't know what they're doing.

LIGURIO: The thing really bothering you must be what you said before: you don't like to lose sight of the Cupola.

MESSER NICIA: You're mistaken! When I was younger I used to travel all the time. Whenever they had a fair at Prato, I always went; and there's not a single village around here that I haven't visited. I can say more than that: I've been to Pisa and Leghorn; so there!

LIGURIO: Then you must have seen the imbecile of Pisa.

MESSER NICIA: You mean the Famous Hill.

LIGURIO: Yes, of course, the Famous Hill. You saw the sea at Leghorn?

MESSER NICIA: Come on, you know I saw it!

LIGURIO: How much bigger is it than the Arno?

MESSER NICIA: What Arno! It's four times the size, more than six, more than seven times—you have no idea. There's nothing to see but water, water, water.

LIGURIO: I'm amazed, then, that a person like yourself, who has dragged his behind all over, should make such a fuss about going to the baths.

MESSER NICIA: You've got the brains of a child! You think it's a joke to have to turn a whole household upside down? Still, my heart is so set on having children that I'd be willing to do almost anything. Listen, you talk to those physicians; find out where they really think I should go. I'll be home with my wife meanwhile, and we can meet later.

LIGURIO: A good idea.

SCENE 3

Ligurio, Callimaco.

LIGURIO: I don't think there's a stupider man in the whole world; and yet what good luck he's had! Money, a beautiful wife, clever, refined, and fit to rule a kingdom. And I don't think there's much truth in that old proverb about marriages that says, "God makes men, they match themselves"—for often you see the best type of man end up with a beast, while, on the other hand, a really sensible woman may get stuck with a madman. But in this fellow's madness there's this advantage, that Callimaco can have something to hope for. But there he is now. What are you doing here, Callimaco?

CALLIMACO: I saw you with the doctor and was waiting for you to leave him so I could find out what you've done.

LIGURIO: You know the kind of man he is: not much sense, less spunk, and he hates to leave Florence. But I warmed him up about it, and he said, finally, that he'd do anything. I think, if we like, we can get him to do what we planned; only, I'm not sure we'll get what we want out of it.

CALLIMACO: Why?

LIGURIO: Who can say! All sorts of people go to those baths, you know; some man might come there who perhaps desires to have Donna Lucrezia as much as you do, and who's richer, more handsome than you; so there's a risk in it of having gone through all this trouble only to benefit others; and it could happen, besides, that having many admirers might make her more difficult—or, if it made her easier, she might still give herself to another, and not to you.

CALLIMACO: You're right, I know. But what can I do then? What action can I take? Where can I turn? I've simply got to try something, and I don't care what it is—huge, dangerous, hurtful, infamous. Better to die than live like this. If I could at least sleep at night, eat, talk to people—if I could find even the slightest pleasure in anything, the strain of waiting might not wear me down so much. But there's no relief here. If my hopes aren't kept up by some possibility of action, it will mean the death of me, one way or another; and with death in sight, I'm not going to be afraid of anything else: I'll try even the most brutal, crude, and vicious thing!

LIGURIO: Don't talk like that! Calm this passion of yours.

CALLIMACO: You can see how I calm it, feeding on these thoughts! That's why either we go through with this and send him to the baths, or we work out another plan that will give me a hope of some kind, even a false one, something to think about, to relieve a little of all this pent-up emotion.

LIGURIO: You're right, and you can count on me.

CALLIMACO: I believe I can, though I'm quite aware that people like you live by duping others. Still, I don't think you're going to be of that sort, for if you tried anything like that and I found out, I'd know how to turn it to my advantage, and you'd immediately lose the use of my house and also the hope of getting what I promised you for the future.

LIGURIO: Don't worry about trusting me; even if I couldn't gain anything by it, as I believe and hope I can, the fact is that I'm beginning to catch the pulse of this thing and I want you to satisfy that desire of yours almost as much as you do. But let's drop all this. The doctor has left it up to me to pick out a physician and to find out which bath is the best one to visit. Now, I want you to do what I'm going to tell you, and that is to say that you've studied medicine and that you've also practiced it for some time in Paris. He'll believe it easily because he's so gullible; and besides, you're a scholar and you can say something to him in Latin.

CALLIMACO: How will that help us?

LIGURIO: It will help us to send him to whatever bath we want, and also to try out another scheme I've been thinking about which is shorter, more certain, more practicable than the baths.

CALLIMACO: What do you mean?

LIGURIO: I mean that if you can get up the nerve, and if you'll trust me, I'll have this whole thing done for you before this time tomorrow. And even if he were the kind of man—which he isn't—to try to find out whether you're really a doctor or not, lack of time, the very nature of the thing, will stop him from asking questions; or, even if he should ask questions, he'll be too late to spoil our plans.

CALLIMACO: You're bringing me back to life; but this promises too much, this makes me hope too much. How will you do it?

LIGURIO: When the time comes you'll find out; there's no point in telling you now; we've hardly enough time to act, much less to talk. Go in the house and wait for me there, and I'll go over to see the doctor; and if I bring him to see you, be sure you follow closely what I say, and go along with it.

CALLIMACO: I'll do it, though I'm afraid the hope you've given me is doomed to go up in smoke.

SONG

He who has never felt your power, Love,
Directs his hopes and fervent prayers above
In vain, for he can never know
The joy of heaven's highest prize;
Or know how one both lives and dies
At once, leaves good behind to go
A ruinous way; nor can he guess
Why one may sometimes love self less
Than others, or how fear and hope can freeze
And grind to nothing every heart they seize.
He knows not why the arms you bear
Fill gods as well as men with fear.

ACT II

SCENE 1

Ligurio, Messer Nicia, Siro.

LIGURIO: As I was saying, I think God has sent us this man, to help you fulfill that desire of yours. He has worked wonders in Paris. And don't be surprised that he hasn't practiced medicine here in Florence; the reason is, first of all, because he's rich, and second, because at any moment he's apt to go back to Paris.

MESSER NICIA: But look here, old friend, that's important. I wouldn't want him to get me all tangled up in this and then leave me high and dry.

LIGURIO: Don't trouble yourself about that: what you have to worry about is that he might not want to take this case; but if he does take it, he won't let go until he has seen it through to the end.

MESSER NICIA: For that side of it, I'll have to rely on you; but as for the scientific side, I'll be the one to tell you, as soon as I talk to him, whether he's a man of real learning—he won't sell me any empty bladders!

LIGURIO: Oh, I know you, all right, and that's why I'm taking you to him now, so that you can talk to him; and after you've talked to him, if he doesn't seem to you, by his presence, his learning, his speech, to be someone you can trust as a baby trusts its mother, tell me I'm not myself!

MESSER NICIA: Then, by all the angels in heaven, it's settled! Let's go. But where does he live?

LIGURIO: He lives up on this square, at that door you see right in front of you.

MESSER NICIA: Let's hurry over there.

16

LIGURIO: (*Knocks*) There you are.

SIRO: (*Within*) Who is it?

LIGURIO: Is Callimaco there?

SIRO: Yes, he is.

MESSER NICIA: Why don't you say "Master" Callimaco?

LIGURIO: He doesn't care about such trifles.

MESSER NICIA: Never mind, do what you're supposed to, and if he doesn't like it, that's his business.

SCENE 2

Callimaco, Messer Nicia, Ligurio.

CALLIMACO: Who is it that wishes to see me?

MESSER NICIA: Bona dies, domine magister.

CALLIMACO: Et vobis, bona, domine doctor.

LIGURIO: (*Aside to* NICIA) What do you think?

MESSER NICIA: (*Aside to* LIGURIO) Excellent, by heaven!

LIGURIO: If you expect me to stay here with you, you'd better talk so that I can understand, otherwise we'll be at cross purposes.

CALLIMACO: And what good business have we?

MESSER NICIA: What shall I say? I'm out looking for two things that someone else would probably try to avoid, and that is, to make trouble for myself and for others. I don't have children, and I want them, and to give myself this trouble I've come to bother you.

CALLIMACO: It could not in the least displease me to do a good turn for you, or for any other good and honest men like yourself. Indeed, I have not studied so hard these many years in Paris except that I might be of service to people like you.

MESSER NICIA: Gran mercè; and should you ever require my professional assistance, I would be most happy to serve you. But let us get back ad rem nostram. Have you decided what bath would be good to make my wife become pregnant? Because I know Ligurio here has told you . . . whatever he may have told you.

CALLIMACO: That's true. But to satisfy your desire, we must know the cause of your wife's sterility, for there may be a number of causes. Nam causae sterilitatis sunt: aut in semine, aut in matrice, aut in instrumentis seminariis, aut in virga, aut in causa extrinsica.

MESSER NICIA: But this is the most remarkable man on earth!

CALLIMACO: It could also be that this sterility is caused by you, because of impotence. In that case, there would be no possible remedy.

MESSER NICIA: Me? Impotent? Oh, you'll make me laugh! I don't think there's a man more vigorous and virile to be found in all Florence!

CALLIMACO: If that's not it, then put your mind at ease, for we'll surely find some remedy.

MESSER NICIA: Isn't there some other kind of remedy besides the baths? I'd rather not have that inconvenience, and my wife would be very reluctant to leave Florence.

LIGURIO: Yes, there is! I want to answer that myself! Callimaco stands too much on ceremony. (To CALLIMACO) Haven't you told me you know how to prepare a certain mixture that can't fail to bring on pregnancy?

CALLIMACO: Yes, I have; but I like to be careful with people I don't know, because I don't want to be mistaken for a quack.

MESSER NICIA: Don't worry about me. You've amazed me so much already that there's nothing I wouldn't believe or do on your advice.

LIGURIO: I think you'll have to examine the specimen.

CALLIMACO: Of course, that's essential.

LIGURIO: Call Siro; have him accompany the doctor home

to get it, and then return here. We'll wait for him in the house.

CALLIMACO: Siro, go with him; and if it suits you, my good sir, come back quickly, and we'll work out something agreeable.

MESSER NICIA: What's that? If it suits me! I'll be back in an instant. I have more faith in you than the Huns have in their swords!

SCENE 3

Messer Nicia, Siro.

MESSER NICIA: This master of yours is a very remarkable man.

SIRO: More than you can say.

MESSER NICIA: The king of France must think highly of him.

SIRO: Very highly.

MESSER NICIA: That must be the reason he likes to live in France.

SIRO: That's what I think.

MESSER NICIA: And he does well. In this country they're all muckworms. They don't appreciate any kind of ability. If he were to stay here nobody would pay attention to him. I ought to know—I worked my guts out to learn my two cents' worth, and if I had to earn a living by it, I'd be out in the cold, believe me.

SIRO: Do you earn a hundred ducats in a year?

MESSER NICIA: Go on—not a hundred lire, not a hundred red pennies even. And that's because in this country people like us, who don't have political pull, can't get a dog to yap after them; we're only good for sitting around at funerals or at wedding parties, or for loafing on the square all day long. (*With bravado*) But I don't bother about them, I don't need anybody. There are plenty worse off who would like to be where I am. (*Suddenly becoming more cautious*) But I wouldn't want anybody to say I said so, otherwise I might really get a heavy fine hung on me, or get stuck with a boil in the rear that'll make me sweat!

SIRO: Don't worry.

MESSER NICIA: We're home. Wait for me here, I'll be right down.

SIRO: Go right ahead.

SCENE 4

Siro.

SIRO: If the other doctors were all like this one, we'd all go crazy. Oh, that rascal Ligurio and that raving master of mine are going to lead him around and bring him to shame, all right! And to be frank, I'd like to see it happen if I could be sure it wouldn't ever leak out. If it does leak out, I'll be in danger of losing my life, and my master, his life and his goods. He has become a physician all of a sudden! But I haven't exactly figured out what their scheme is, or where this deception of theirs is heading. . . . But there's the doctor coming out with a chamber pot in his hand. Who wouldn't laugh at that old buzzard!

SCENE 5

Messer Nicia, Siro.

MESSER NICIA: (*Muttering to himself*) I've always done things your way; this I want you to do my way! If I could have known I wasn't going to have any children, I would have done better to marry some peasant girl. Is that you there, Siro? Come on, after me. What trouble I had to go through to get that silly wife of mine to give me this specimen; and it isn't as if she wasn't anxious to have children, for she's more concerned about it than I am; but the minute I ask her to do some little thing, it's always a big argument.

SIRO: Be patient. You have to go easy with women to make them do what you want.

MESSER NICIA: What easy! She makes me sick! Run ahead, tell your master and Ligurio that I'm here.

SIRO: They're coming out now.

SCENE 6

Ligurio, Callimaco, Messer Nicia.

LIGURIO: (*Aside to* CALLIMACO) The doctor can be persuaded easily; the only difficulty is the woman, and we'll find a way around that.

CALLIMACO: (*To* MESSER NICIA) Do you have the specimen?

MESSER NICIA: Siro has it underneath there.

CALLIMACO: Let me have it. Ah ha! This specimen seems to show kidney trouble.

MESSER NICIA: It does look a little murky; and yet she just did it.

CALLIMACO: Don't let that surprise you. Nam mulieris urinae sunt semper maioris glossitiei et albedinis, et minoris pulchritudinis, quam virorum. Huius autem, in caetera, causa est amplitudo canalium, mixtio eorum quae ex matrice exeunt cum urina.

MESSER NICIA: Pots of San Puccio! This fellow rubs me smooth as silk! Just listen to the way he talks about these things!

CALLIMACO: I'm afraid this woman, here, is not covered well at night, and that's why the urine comes out crude like this.

MESSER NICIA: She even has a heavy quilt to keep on top of her! But she stays on her knees half the night stringing off paternosters before she comes to bed, and she can take the cold like a beast.

CALLIMACO: The point is, doctor: either you place your trust in me or you don't; either I'm to go ahead with this and give you a sure remedy, or not. For my part, I'm going to give you the remedy; if you trust me, you'll take it. And if a year from today your wife isn't holding a child of her own in her arms, I'll hold myself bound to give you two thousand ducats.

MESSER NICIA: Please go on, for I'm ready to accept your help with all my heart and to trust you more than my own confessor.

CALLIMACO: You have to understand this, that there is no surer way to make a woman pregnant than to have her drink a potion made of the mandragola. This is something I have tested again and again, always with positive results; and if it were not for this, the queen of France would be sterile, and countless other noble ladies of that kingdom.

MESSER NICIA: Is it possible?

CALLIMACO: It is exactly as I've said. And fortune has been very kind to you, in that I happen to have brought with me, here, all the things that have to be put in that mixture, and you can have them whenever you wish.

MESSER NICIA: When would she have to take it?

CALLIMACO: Tonight after supper, because the moon is in its right phase and the time couldn't be more propitious.

MESSER NICIA: That's not such a big thing; by all means prepare it, and I'll make her take it.

CALLIMACO: And now we have to consider this also, that the man who is with her first, after she has taken this potion, dies within a week; and you couldn't save him for the world!

MESSER NICIA: Puke! I don't want any of this slimy business.

You're not going to stick me in it! You've fixed me good, all right!

CALLIMACO: Pull yourself together; there's a remedy.

MESSER NICIA: What?

CALLIMACO: Get someone else to sleep with her at once, who will draw to himself—being with her a whole night—the full infection of the mandragola. After that you can lie there without danger.

MESSER NICIA: I don't want to do this.

CALLIMACO: Why?

MESSER NICIA: Because I don't want to turn my wife into a bitch and make myself a cuckold!

CALLIMACO: What are you saying, doctor? I see you're not the wise sort of man I took you for. So you are going to hesitate to do what the king of France has done, and all the noblemen over there?

MESSER NICIA: Who do you expect me to get to do such a crazy thing? If I tell him about it, he won't want to do it; if I don't tell him, I'm betraying him, and that's a case for the Grand Jury. I don't want to get in trouble on account of this!

CALLIMACO: If that's the only thing bothering you, leave it to me.

MESSER NICIA: How will we go about it?

CALLIMACO: I'll tell you: I'll give you the potion tonight after supper; you make her drink it and put her to bed right away, when it's about ten o'clock. Then we'll disguise ourselves —you, Ligurio, Siro, and myself—and we'll go search in the new market, in the old market, in places like that; and the first young rascal we find loafing about, we'll gag him and, with the help of a few good whacks, we'll march him into the house, and into your room, in the dark. We'll put him to bed, we'll tell him what he has to do; and there won't be any trouble at all. Then, in the morning, you'll send him off before day breaks, you'll make your wife bathe, you'll be with her as it pleases you, and without any danger.

MESSER NICIA: I'll agree, since you tell me that kings and princes and noblemen have done it this way; but above all, don't ever let it be known—for the Grand Jury's sake!

CALLIMACO: Who in the world would say anything?

MESSER NICIA: There's one more task, and it's important.

CALLIMACO: What?

MESSER NICIA: Get my wife to agree, which I don't think she'll ever be willing to do.

CALLIMACO: You're right, certainly; but I wouldn't want to remain her husband another minute if I couldn't make her do what I want.

LIGURIO: I've got the answer!

MESSER NICIA: How?

LIGURIO: Through her confessor.

CALLIMACO: (*Aside to* LIGURIO) Who will get the confessor to do it?

LIGURIO: (*Aside to* CALLIMACO) You, me, money, our wickedness, theirs.

MESSER NICIA: I'm afraid, to say the least, that if I tell her, she won't want to speak to her confessor.

LIGURIO: I have an answer for that, too.

CALLIMACO: Tell me!

LIGURIO: Get her mother to take her.

MESSER NICIA: She listens to her. . . .

LIGURIO: And I know that her mother sees things our way. Come, let's hurry it up, because it's getting late. Callimaco, you go for a stroll and make sure that, two hours from now, we can find you at home with the potion all ready. We'll go over to see the mother—the doctor and I, since I know her pretty well—and we'll try to persuade her; then we'll call on the friar, and we'll report back to you what we've done.

CALLIMACO: (*Aside to* LIGURIO) Wait, don't leave me alone!

LIGURIO: You look like a cooked goose!

CALLIMACO: Where am I supposed to go now?

LIGURIO: Here, there, up this street, down that one: Florence is a big place!

CALLIMACO: I'm as good as dead!

SONG

It's plain for everyone to see
How happy a born fool must be,
Believing everything he hears.
Ambition never moves him, fears
Don't weigh him down—which are the chief
Seeds of man's suffering and grief.
Our doctor, here, would not suspect a lie
If he were told that jackasses can fly;
He has his heart so set on fatherhood,
That he's forgotten every other good.

ACT III

SCENE 1

Sostrata, Messer Nicia, Ligurio.

SOSTRATA: I've always heard it said that it's a wise person's duty to choose the best course among the worst. If you can't have children in any other way, then this way ought to be taken—as long as it doesn't weigh on the conscience.

MESSER NICIA: That's the truth.

LIGURIO: Now you go to see your daughter; Messer Nicia and I will look for Friar Timoteo, her confessor, and we'll describe the whole situation to him, so that you won't have to do it. Then you'll hear what he has to say.

SOSTRATA: That's how we'll do it. Your way is off there; I'll find Lucrezia, and I'll see to it that she goes to talk to the friar.

SCENE 2

Messer Nicia, Ligurio.

MESSER NICIA: You're probably surprised, Ligurio, that we have to make such a long story of it to convince my wife; but if you knew the rest of it, you wouldn't be surprised.

LIGURIO: I think it may be because all women are naturally suspicious.

MESSER NICIA: No, it's not that. She used to be the sweetest person in the world, and easy to handle. But when a neighbor of hers told her that she would become pregnant if she vowed to attend the first mass of the Servi for forty mornings, she

26

made the vow, and she went maybe twenty mornings. Well, would you believe it, that one of those fat friars started sniffing around her, so that she wouldn't go back there any more? It's really a shame, you know, when those who should set good examples for us turn out to be like that. Am I right or not?

LIGURIO: What! By the devil, you certainly are!

MESSER NICIA: Since that time she's had her ears perked like a rabbit; and the minute anything is said to her, she finds a thousand excuses.

LIGURIO: I'm not surprised any more. But, that vow—how was it fulfilled?

MESSER NICIA: She got a dispensation.

LIGURIO: Good. But let me have twenty-five ducats, if you have them, because in situations like this money has to be spent; you have to get this friar to be your friend right away, and give him something better to hope for.

MESSER NICIA: Here, take them; that doesn't bother me. I'll stock up somewhere else.

LIGURIO: These friars are cunning, shrewd; and it's understandable, since they know all our sins as well as their own; someone who has had no experience with them could easily make a mistake and not know how to get them to do what he wants. The point is that I wouldn't want you to spoil everything by talking, since a man of your caliber, who stays in his study all day long, understands his books but often doesn't know how to deal with worldly matters. (*Aside*) This fellow is so stupid I really am afraid he'll spoil everything.

MESSER NICIA: Tell me what you want me to do.

LIGURIO: You let me do the talking; don't you talk at all unless I give you a sign.

MESSER NICIA: Very well. What sign will you make?

LIGURIO: I'll wink an eye; I'll bite my lip. No, no! let's do it another way. How long has it been since you talked to the friar?

MESSER NICIA: It's over ten years.

LIGURIO: Good. I'll tell him you've become deaf and you won't answer, you won't say a word unless we speak very loudly.

MESSER NICIA: I'll do it.

LIGURIO: Don't let it bother you if I say anything that seems to go against what we want, because it'll all turn out as it should in the end.

MESSER NICIA: Patience!

SCENE 3

Friar Timoteo, Woman.

FRIAR TIMOTEO: If you want me to hear your confession, I will do as you wish.

WOMAN: Not today. I have an appointment. It's enough to have let off a little steam just standing here like this. Have you said those masses to Our Lady?

FRIAR TIMOTEO: Yes, madam.

WOMAN: Here, take this florin then, and every Monday, for the next two months, say a memorial mass for my husband's soul. Even though he was a wretch, still the flesh pulls; I can't help feeling something every time I think about it. But do you think he's in Purgatory?

FRIAR TIMOTEO: Undoubtedly.

WOMAN: I'm not so sure. You know what he used to do to me sometimes. Oh! how many times I brought my complaints to you about it! I would avoid him as much as I could, but he was so importunate! Uh! Good Lord. . . .

FRIAR TIMOTEO: Rest assured, God's mercy abounds. If a man has the will, he will never lack the time to repent.

WOMAN: Do you think the Turks will invade Italy this year?

FRIAR TIMOTEO: If you don't keep up your devotions, yes.

WOMAN: Good heavens! God help us with such devilish things! I'm terribly afraid of that impaling they do. . . . But I see a woman in church who has a spool of yarn that belongs to me. I want to see her. Have a good day.

FRIAR TIMOTEO: Good-by.

SCENE 4

Friar Timoteo, Ligurio, Messer Nicia.

FRIAR TIMOTEO: Women are the most generous creatures in the world, and the most troublesome. If you chase them away you rid yourself of the troubles but also of the advantages; if you encourage them, you have advantages and troubles together. It's the old saying: you can't have honey without flies. —And what are you after, my good sirs? Do I not see Messer Nicia?

LIGURIO: Speak loudly, for he has become so deaf that he can no longer hear anything.

FRIAR TIMOTEO: I'm glad to see you.

LIGURIO: Louder.

FRIAR TIMOTEO: Glad to see you.

MESSER NICIA: Glad to find you, Father.

FRIAR TIMOTEO: And what are you after?

MESSER NICIA: Very well, thank you.

LIGURIO: You'd better speak to me, Father, because to make him hear you'll have to turn this whole square into an uproar.

FRIAR TIMOTEO: What do you want from me?

LIGURIO: Messer Nicia here and another gentleman whose name you'll learn later have several hundred ducats they want to have distributed as alms.

MESSER NICIA: Puke!

LIGURIO: (*Aside to* NICIA) Quiet, damn you! It won't be much! (*To* FRIAR TIMOTEO) Don't be surprised at anything he says, Father, for he doesn't hear but sometimes he thinks he does, and then his answers don't make sense.

FRIAR TIMOTEO: Please continue, and let him say anything he wants.

LIGURIO:—Of which money I have a part with me; and they have decided that you should be the one to distribute it.

FRIAR TIMOTEO: I'll be very glad to.

LIGURIO: But before these alms can be given, it will be necessary for you to help us in a rather unusual situation involving Messer Nicia here—and only you can help—in which the honor of his whole family is at stake.

FRIAR TIMOTEO: What is it?

LIGURIO: I don't know whether or not you ever met Cammillo Calfucci, the nephew of our Messer Nicia here.

FRIAR TIMOTEO: Yes, I've met him.

LIGURIO: This man had to go to France on some business last year, and not having a wife—for she had died—he left a daughter of marriageable age in the care of a convent, the name of which I don't have to tell you just now.

FRIAR TIMOTEO: What happened?

LIGURIO: What happened was that either through the nuns' carelessness or the girl's foolishness, she is now four months pregnant, so that if the matter is not patched up wisely, the doctor, the nuns, the girl, Cammillo, the whole Calfucci household are disgraced; and the doctor is so concerned about this scandal that he has vowed (if it doesn't come to light) to give three hundred ducats for the love of God.

MESSER NICIA: That's gibberish!

LIGURIO: (*Aside to* NICIA) Be quiet! (*Continuing*) And he will give them through your hands. Only you and the abbess can straighten things out.

FRIAR TIMOTEO: How?

LIGURIO: Persuade the abbess to give the girl some potion to make her miscarry.

FRIAR TIMOTEO: That's something that needs to be thought about.

LIGURIO: Look how much good will result from doing this: you'll be saving the reputation of the convent, of the girl, of the relatives; you'll be restoring a maid to her father; you'll be satisfying Messer Nicia here and his many relatives; you'll be giving out as much alms as you can give with three hundred ducats; and, on the other side, the offense is only to a piece of unborn, senseless flesh that might well be lost in a thousand ways. And I believe the really good things are those that do good for the greatest number, and in which the greatest number find satisfaction.

FRIAR TIMOTEO: So be it, in God's name. Let it be done as you wish, and all done for God's sake and for charity. Tell me what convent it is, give me the potion and, if you see fit, this money here, so that we can start to do some good.

LIGURIO: Now you seem to me to be the man of religion I thought you were. Take this part of the money. The name of the convent is. . . . But wait, there's a woman in church beckoning to me; I'll be right back. Don't leave Messer Nicia; I only want to say a few words to her.

SCENE 5

Friar Timoteo, Messer Nicia.

FRIAR TIMOTEO: This girl, how old is she?

MESSER NICIA: I'm dumbfounded!

FRIAR TIMOTEO: I say, how old is this girl?

MESSER NICIA: (*Looking after* LIGURIO) May God put a curse on him!

FRIAR TIMOTEO: Why?

MESSER NICIA: So that he'll have it!

FRIAR TIMOTEO: (*Aside*) It looks like I've slipped into a pit!

I'm dealing with one man that's mad and another that's deaf.
One runs away; the other can't hear. But if these coins aren't
cheap slugs, I'll be making out better than they will! Here is
Ligurio coming back.

SCENE 6

Ligurio, Friar Timoteo, Messer Nicia.

LIGURIO: (*Aside to* NICIA) Keep quiet, Messere. (*To* FRIAR
TIMOTEO) Oh, I have some great news, Father!

FRIAR TIMOTEO: What?

LIGURIO: That woman I just spoke to told me that the girl
in question miscarried by herself.

FRIAR TIMOTEO: (*Muttering*) Fine! And there go the alms
like lard on the fire!

LIGURIO: What did you say?

FRIAR TIMOTEO: I said that you have all the more reason
now for giving these alms.

LIGURIO: The alms will be given whenever you want; but it
will be necessary to do another thing for the doctor here.

FRIAR TIMOTEO: And what is that?

LIGURIO: Something less weighty, less scandalous, more
agreeable to us, more advantageous to you.

FRIAR TIMOTEO: What is it? I'm under obligation to you,
and I seem to have reached such a level of familiarity that
there's nothing I would not do.

LIGURIO: I'd rather tell you about it in church, just between
the two of us; the doctor won't mind waiting out there. We'll
be right back.

MESSER NICIA: Go to the devil and good riddance!

FRIAR TIMOTEO: Let us go.

SCENE 7

Messer Nicia.

MESSER NICIA: Is it day or night? Am I awake or dreaming? Maybe I'm drunk, although I haven't taken a drink yet today to keep up with all this gibberish. We agree to tell the friar one thing and he tells him another, then he wants me to play deaf. I would have had to plug up my ears like the Dane not to hear all the crazy things he said—and to what purpose, God only knows! I'm out twenty-five ducats and my business hasn't even been mentioned yet. And now they've left me stuck here like a pretzel on a stick. But here they come; damn the pair of them, if they haven't discussed my business!

SCENE 8

Friar Timoteo, Ligurio, Messer Nicia.

FRIAR TIMOTEO: Then let the women come. I know what I must do and, if my authority means anything, we'll have this match made before the night is over.

LIGURIO: Messer Nicia, Friar Timoteo is ready to help us in everything; we'll have to wait now for the women to get here.

MESSER NICIA: Oh, you make me tingle with happiness all over. Will it be a boy?

LIGURIO: A boy.

MESSER NICIA: I'm so happy I could cry.

FRIAR TIMOTEO: Go into the church, I'll wait for the women here. Stay over to one side, so that they don't see you. As soon as they leave, I'll tell you what they've said. (NICIA *and* LIGURIO *go into the church*.)

SCENE 9

Friar Timoteo.

FRIAR TIMOTEO: I'm not sure who's tricked whom. This rascal Ligurio came to me with that first story just to try me out, for if I had not consented to it he would not have told me about this, not wanting to reveal their plans without advantage; and, of course, they didn't care about that fake story. I have to admit I've been tricked; still, this trick has a certain advantage in it for me. Messer Nicia and Callimaco are rich, and from each of them, for different reasons, I should be able to squeeze out plenty. The thing is bound to be kept secret for they no more want it known than I do. Whatever happens, I won't be sorry; though I'm afraid there may be some difficulty, since Donna Lucrezia is a good and prudent woman. But I'll get at her on the matter of kindness. Women are all short on brains, anyway, and if one of them can tell you two things straight, it's something to preach about, for among the blind one eye is enough to make a king. But here she comes with her mother, who is a regular beast of a woman and will be a big help to me in getting the daughter to do what I want.

SCENE 10

Sostrata, Lucrezia.

SOSTRATA: I do believe that you believe me, my dear child, when I say that I value your honor as much as any person in the world, and that I would never advise you to do something that wasn't proper. I have told you, and I'm telling you again, that if Friar Timoteo tells you there's nothing in it to weigh on the conscience, then you should do it and not worry about it.

LUCREZIA: I've always been afraid that Messer Nicia's long-ing to have children would make us do something absurd; and that's why, whenever he has spoken to me about anything, I've been suspicious and hesitant about it, especially after what you know happened to me for having gone to the Servi. But of all the things that have ever been tried, I think this is the strang-est—that I should have to submit my body to this outrage, and to be the cause of a man's death for outraging me. For I couldn't believe it, even if I were the last woman left in the world, and the whole human race had to start all over again from me—that I would be expected to do such a thing.

SOSTRATA: I don't know how to tell you a lot of things, my child. You'll talk to the Friar, you'll see what he tells you and then you'll do what you're advised to do by him, by us, and by those who really love you.

LUCREZIA: I'm sweating with rage.

SCENE 11

Friar Timoteo, Lucrezia, Sostrata.

FRIAR TIMOTEO: Welcome, my dear ladies. I know what it is that you want to learn from me, for Messer Nicia has al-ready spoken to me about it. Indeed, I have been bent over my books for more than two hours, studying this matter; and after careful examination I have found many things that, both in particular and in general, stand in our favor.

LUCREZIA: Are you talking seriously, or in jest?

FRIAR TIMOTEO: Ah, Donna Lucrezia, is this anything to jest about? Am I still a stranger to you?

LUCREZIA: No, Father; but this seems to me the strangest thing anyone ever heard of.

FRIAR TIMOTEO: Madonna, I understand how you feel, but I must ask you to say no more about it. There are many things which at a distance seem terrible, unbearable, strange; and then when you approach them they turn out to be very human, quite bearable, familiar. That's why there is the saying that the fears are worse than the misfortunes; this is an instance of it.

LUCREZIA: God be willing!

FRIAR TIMOTEO: Let me get back to what I was saying. As far as the conscience goes, you have to bear in mind this general principle, that, when confronted with a good that is certain and an evil that is uncertain, one must never renounce that good for fear of that evil. Here we have a good that is certain: you will become pregnant, you will win a soul for our Good Lord; the uncertain evil is that the one who, after the potion, lies with you will die—but it also happens that some do not die. Still, since the thing is doubtful, it is well for Messer Nicia not to run that risk. As for the act itself, to call it a sin is empty talk; for it is the will that sins, not the body. What makes it sinful is to displease the husband, and you please him; to take pleasure in it, and you find only displeasure. Besides, it is the end that must be considered in all things; the end for you is to fill a throne in Heaven, to make your husband happy. The Bible says that the daughters of Lot, believing themselves to be the sole surviving women in the world, mated with their father, and because their intention was good, they did not sin.

LUCREZIA: What are you trying to persuade me to do?

SOSTRATA: Let him persuade you, my child. Can't you see that a woman that has no children has no home? When her husband dies she's left like a beast, abandoned by everyone.

FRIAR TIMOTEO: I swear to you, Madonna, by this consecrated breast, that to yield to your husband in this will weigh on the conscience no more than eating meat on Wednesday, which is a sin that is washed away with holy water.

LUCREZIA: What are you leading me into, Father?

FRIAR TIMOTEO: I'm leading you to such things that you will always have reason to pray to God in my behalf; and next year, you will have fuller satisfaction than now.

SOSTRATA: She'll do what you want. I will put her to bed myself tonight. What are you afraid of, you ninny? There are at least fifty women in this city who would raise their hands to heaven for this!

LUCREZIA: Very well—but I can never believe I'll be alive tomorrow morning.

FRIAR TIMOTEO: Don't worry, my child. I will pray God for you; I will recite the prayer of the Angel Raphael, that he stay by your side. Go quickly and prepare for this mystery, for it is getting late.

SOSTRATA: Farewell, Father.

LUCREZIA: God help me, and Our Lady! May they keep me from harm! (*The women leave.*)

SCENE 12

Friar Timoteo, Ligurio, Messer Nicia.

FRIAR TIMOTEO: Oh, Ligurio, come out here.

LIGURIO: How is it going?

FRIAR TIMOTEO: Well. They've gone home, ready to do everything, and there won't be any difficulty because her mother is going to stay with her and wants to put her to bed herself.

MESSER NICIA: Is that the truth?

FRIAR TIMOTEO: Well, well, your deafness is cured!

LIGURIO: St. Clement has answered his prayers.

FRIAR TIMOTEO: I should set up a votive plaque for you to get you a little publicity, since I have shared this good fortune with you.

MESSER NICIA: We're getting off the subject. Will my wife raise any difficulty about doing what I want?

FRIAR TIMOTEO: No, I tell you.

MESSER NICIA: I'm the happiest man in the world!

FRIAR TIMOTEO: I should think so. You'll get yourself a baby boy out of it, and let him who has not, do without.

LIGURIO: Go back to your prayers, friar, and if we should need anything else, we'll come for you. Messer Nicia, you go to her, to keep her firm in this decision, and I will look for Master Callimaco to make sure he sends the potion; and be sure you're at hand at seven o'clock to plan what has to be done at ten.

MESSER NICIA: That's the idea; good-by.

FRIAR TIMOTEO: God keep you.

SONG

How pleasant to pursue deceit
To its envisioned dearest goal!
It makes all bitterness turn sweet
And lightens every troubled soul.
O remedy of highest worth,
Man's surest guide on earth,
When you, with your great strength, give others joy,
You thereby make love rich; and you destroy
The spell of poison, stone, or evil sign
With but the saintly counsels you design.

ACT IV

SCENE 1

Callimaco.

CALLIMACO: I can't wait to find out what those fellows have done! Can it be that Ligurio won't show up? Here it is—not the eleventh, mind you, but the twelfth hour! What a terrible nervous strain this has been, and is! It's certainly true that fortune and nature balance their accounts: if anything good happens to you, something bad is bound to spring up right after it. The more my hope has increased, the more my fear has increased. Poor me! How can I possibly live through such anguish, tormented by these fears and hopes? I'm a ship harassed by two contrary winds that is seized with greater and greater fear the closer it gets to port. The simple-mindedness of Messer Nicia makes me hope; the foresight and firmness of Lucrezia fill me with fear. The worst misery is that I find no peace anywhere. Sometimes I try to get control of myself; I scold myself for this madness and say: What are you doing? Have you gone mad? Suppose you get what you want, what of it? You'll see your mistake; you'll be sorry you took so much trouble and worried so much about it. Don't you know how little good is actually found in the things a man desires compared with what a man expects to find? On the other side of it, the worst that can happen to you is that you should die and go to hell for it; but so many others have died—hell is full of nice people; are you going to be ashamed to go there? Face your lot; fly from misfortune, but when you can't fly from it, bear it like a man. Don't debase yourself, don't be cowardly like a woman. And in that way I console myself, but it doesn't last long, for I'm pressed on all sides by such a desire to be with that woman at least once that from the soles of my feet

39

up to my head I feel myself dissolving; my legs shake, my stomach turns upside down; my heart pounds itself loose from my chest, my arms hang limp; my voice is lost, my eyes are dazed, my head spins. At least if I could find Ligurio I could get some relief talking to him. But here he is, hurrying toward me; the news he brings will either give me a few more hours of life, or kill me outright.

SCENE 2

Ligurio, Callimaco.

LIGURIO: (*To the audience*) I have never been more anxious to find Callimaco and have never had more trouble finding him. If I were bringing him bad news I would have run into him at once. I've been to his house, on the square, in the market place, at the terrace of the Spini, at the portico of the Tornaquinci, and haven't found him. These lovers have quicksilver under their feet; they can't hold still.

CALLIMACO: (*To the audience*) There goes Ligurio, turning this way and that; he must be looking for me. What's holding me? Why don't I call to him? He seems cheerful enough. Oh, Ligurio, Ligurio!

LIGURIO: Oh, Callimaco, where have you been?

CALLIMACO: What news?

LIGURIO: Good.

CALLIMACO: Good, really?

LIGURIO: The best!

CALLIMACO: Is Lucrezia willing?

LIGURIO: Yes.

CALLIMACO: Did the friar do what he was supposed to?

LIGURIO: He did.

CALLIMACO: Oh, blessed monk! From now on I will always pray to God for him.

LIGURIO: Oh fine! As if bad things, as well as good, can come by God's grace! The friar will want something other than prayers.

CALLIMACO: What will he want?

LIGURIO: Money.

CALLIMACO: We'll give it to him. How much have you promised him?

LIGURIO: Three hundred ducats.

CALLIMACO: You have done well.

LIGURIO: The doctor has shelled out twenty-five.

CALLIMACO: How come?

LIGURIO: He shelled them out—never mind the reason.

CALLIMACO: What did Lucrezia's mother do?

LIGURIO: Almost everything. As soon as she heard that her daughter was to have this good night without sin, she never stopped pleading, ordering, encouraging Lucrezia until she succeeded in taking her to the friar, and there she worked on her in such a way that she finally consented.

CALLIMACO: Oh God, what have I ever done to deserve such blessings? I could almost die for joy!

LIGURIO: What kind of man is this? One time for joy, another time for sorrow, this fellow is bent on dying, no matter what! Have you got the potion ready?

CALLIMACO: Yes, I have.

LIGURIO: What will you send him?

CALLIMACO: A glass of Hypocras—just the thing to settle the stomach and cheer up the head. Oh, oh damn it all, I'm ruined!

LIGURIO: What is it? (*To the audience*) What can it be?

CALLIMACO: There's no way out.

LIGURIO: What the devil is the matter?

CALLIMACO: Nothing has been settled. I've walled myself in.

LIGURIO: Why? Why don't you speak up? Take your hands away from your face.

CALLIMACO: Don't you realize I told Messer Nicia that you, he, Siro, and I would catch someone to tuck in next to his wife?

LIGURIO: What of it?

CALLIMACO: What do you mean, what of it? If I'm with you, I can't be the one who is caught; if I'm not there, he'll realize it's a trick.

LIGURIO: You're right. But can't we work something?

CALLIMACO: No, I don't see how.

LIGURIO: Yes, there's a way!

CALLIMACO: What?

LIGURIO: Let me think about it for a moment.

CALLIMACO: That clears up everything! If you've got to think about it now, I'm finished.

LIGURIO: I've got it!

CALLIMACO: What?

LIGURIO: I'll get the friar, who has helped us this far, to help us the rest of the way.

CALLIMACO: How?

LIGURIO: We all have to disguise ourselves; I'll get the friar to put on a disguise; he'll alter his voice, his face, his clothes; and I'll tell the doctor that it's you. He'll believe it.

CALLIMACO: I like that; but what will I be doing?

LIGURIO: I want you to put on a tattered cloak and come around the corner of his house carrying a lute and singing a little song.

CALLIMACO: With my face showing?

LIGURIO: Yes, for if you were to wear a mask he would become suspicious.

CALLIMACO: He'll recognize me.

LIGURIO: No, he won't, because I want you to twist your face, to open, screw up, or stretch back your mouth, squint an eye. Let's see you try it.

CALLIMACO: Should I do it like this?

LIGURIO: No.

CALLIMACO: Like this?

LIGURIO: Not enough.

CALLIMACO: This way?

LIGURIO: Yes, yes; keep that in mind. I have a nose at home; I want you to stick it on.

CALLIMACO: Very well, and then what?

LIGURIO: As soon as you appear on the corner, we'll be there, we'll snatch away your lute, grab you, spin you around, take you into the house, put you to bed; the rest you'll have to do for yourself.

CALLIMACO: The thing is to get there.

LIGURIO: You'll get there, but to work it so that you can return is up to you, not us.

CALLIMACO: How?

LIGURIO: Win her tonight, and, before leaving, tell her who you are, reveal the trick to her, show her your love for her, tell her how much you like her, and how, with no disgrace to herself, she can be your friend and only with much disgrace your enemy. It isn't possible that she won't go along with you and that she should want this night to be the only one.

CALLIMACO: You think so?

LIGURIO: I'm certain of it. But we musn't waste any more time; it's already eight o'clock. Call Siro, send the potion to Messer Nicia, and wait for me in the house. I'll get the friar; I'll make him put on a disguise, bring him here, then we'll get the doctor to do what remains to be done.

CALLIMACO: That's fine. Go right ahead.

SCENE 3

Callimaco, Siro.

CALLIMACO: Oh, Siro!

SIRO: Sir?

CALLIMACO: Come here.

SIRO: Yes, sir.

CALLIMACO: Get that silver goblet out of my bedroom closet and bring it to me covered with a piece of cloth—and be sure you don't spill it along the way.

SIRO: Very well. (*Leaves the room.*)

CALLIMACO: This fellow has been with me ten years and he has always served me faithfully; I think even in this situation I can trust him, and though I haven't told him about this ruse, he must have guessed what it is, for he's a smart rascal and I notice how easily he gets into step.

SIRO: (*Re-enters the room*) Here it is.

CALLIMACO: Good. Now run, quickly, go to Messer Nicia's house and tell him this is the medicine for his wife to take right after supper, and that the earlier she eats supper the better, and that we'll be on the corner as planned, at the time he says he'll be there. Go on, hurry.

SIRO: I will.

CALLIMACO: Listen—if he wants you to wait, then wait, and come back with him; if not, then you come back here to me as soon as you've given him this and after you've told him what I just said.

SIRO: Yes, sir.

SCENE 4

Callimaco.

CALLIMACO: (*To the audience*) I am waiting for Ligurio to get here with the friar; and, believe me, anybody who says that waiting is a hard thing is telling the truth. I'm losing ten pounds every hour thinking of where I am now and of where I may be two hours from now, fearing that something may suddenly happen to upset my whole plan; if that should happen this would be the last night of my life, for I'll either throw myself in the Arno, or I'll hang myself, or I'll fling myself out of those windows, or I'll stab myself on her doorstep. Something or other like that I'm bound to do, to end it all. But is that Ligurio? Yes, it's he. He has someone with him who looks hunchbacked, lame; that must be the friar in disguise. Oh, these friars! If you know one you know them all. Who is that other one approaching them? It looks like Siro, who must have already given my message to the doctor; yes, that's who it is. I'll wait for them here to arrange things with them.

SCENE 5

Siro, Ligurio, Callimaco, Friar Timoteo.

SIRO: Who's that with you, Ligurio?

LIGURIO: A respectable person.

SIRO: Is he really lame or faking?

LIGURIO: Mind your business!

SIRO: Oh, he looks like a real scoundrel!

LIGURIO: Sh! Be quiet! You're messing up everything. Where is Callimaco?

CALLIMACO: Here I am. Welcome.

LIGURIO: Oh, Callimaco, say something to this nut-head Siro. He's already blabbered more than enough nonsense!

CALLIMACO: Listen, Siro, tonight you have to do everything Ligurio tells you to do, and when he gives you an order, obey him as if it came from me; and whatever you see, hear, or notice, keep it absolutely secret, if you value my wealth, my honor, my life, and your own good.

SIRO: I'll do as you say.

CALLIMACO: Did you give the glass to the doctor?

SIRO: Yes, sir.

CALLIMACO: What did he say?

SIRO: That he'll do everything as agreed.

FRIAR TIMOTEO: Is this Callimaco?

CALLIMACO: I am at your service. Our conditions have been settled; you can dispose of me and of all my wealth as of yourself.

FRIAR TIMOTEO: So I've been told, and I believe it, and have undertaken to do for you what I would not have done for any other man in the world.

CALLIMACO: Your efforts won't go to waste.

FRIAR TIMOTEO: I ask nothing more than your good favor.

LIGURIO: Let's drop these formalities. We're going to disguise ourselves, Siro and I. You, Callimaco, come with us, so that you can attend to your business; the friar will wait for us here; we'll be right back, and we'll go to meet Messer Nicia.

CALLIMACO: Right. Let's go.

FRIAR TIMOTEO: I'll wait here.

SCENE 6

Friar Timoteo.

FRIAR TIMOTEO: There's truth in the old saying that bad company leads men to the gallows; and often a person gets into trouble as much for being too easygoing and good-natured as for being too vicious. God knows I had no intention of harming anybody: I kept to my cell, I recited my office, I tended my flock; then this devil of a Ligurio crossed my path, who got me to stick a finger in a mess, into which I've sunk my whole arm, and my whole body, and I still don't know where I'll end up. But my one consolation is that when there are many people involved in a thing, many have to look after it. But here's Ligurio and that servant coming back.

SCENE 7

Friar Timoteo, Ligurio, Siro.

FRIAR TIMOTEO: Welcome back.

LIGURIO: Do we look all right?

FRIAR TIMOTEO: Fine.

LIGURIO: The doctor is not here. We'd better go toward his house; it's after nine o'clock. Let's hurry.

SIRO: Who's opening his door? Is it the servant?

LIGURIO: No, it's him. Ha! Ha! Ha!

SIRO: You're laughing?

LIGURIO: Who wouldn't laugh? He has on a little cloak that barely covers his behind. What the devil has he got on his head? It looks like one of those furred hoods the monks wear. And a small sword underneath. Ah ha! He's muttering I don't know what. Let's stand over to one side and we'll hear of some abuse he has had to suffer from his wife.

SCENE 8

Messer Nicia, Ligurio, Friar Timoteo, Siro, Callimaco.

MESSER NICIA: What a fuss this crazy wife of mine has made! She sent the maid to her mother's house, and the servant to the farm. I praise her for that; but I can't praise her for being so squeamish before she finally agreed to get into bed. "I won't. . . . What will I do. . . . What are you making me do. . . . Dear me! Mamma, Mamma!" And if her mother hadn't given her a piece of her mind, she wouldn't have gotten into that bed! I hope she gets a bellyache! I don't mind women being finicky, but not that much! She's driven us out of our minds, that chicken brain! Then if someone said the cleverest woman of Florence deserves to be hung, she would say: What have I ever done to you?—All I know is that the parade is going to get into town, and before I'm through with this game I'll be able to say with Monna Ghinga: I saw to it with these very hands. (*He struts a little, as if before a mirror*) I look all right! Who would recognize me? I look taller, younger, more slender; there isn't a woman who would charge me bed money. But where can I find those fellows?

LIGURIO: Good evening, Messere.

MESSER NICIA: (*Stepping back*) Oh, eh, eh!

LIGURIO: Don't be afraid; it's only us.

MESSER NICIA: Oh, you're all here. If I hadn't recognized you right away I'd have let you have it straight through with this sword. You're Ligurio? And you, Siro? And this other one, the master?

LIGURIO: (*Trying to hide* FRIAR TIMOTEO) Yes, Messere.

MESSER NICIA: Move aside. Oh, he's disguised himself well, no one could recognize him. Move aside, will you?

LIGURIO: I made him put a couple of nuts in his mouth so he wouldn't be recognized by his voice.

MESSER NICIA: You're really stupid!

LIGURIO: Why?

MESSER NICIA: Why didn't you tell me earlier? I would have put a couple in my mouth, too. You know how important it is not to be recognized by the voice.

LIGURIO: Here, put this in your mouth.

MESSER NICIA: What is it?

LIGURIO: A ball of wax.

MESSER NICIA: Give it to me. Ca, pu, ca, co, co. Blast you, you dumb ox!

LIGURIO: Oh, I'm sorry! I gave you something else instead, by mistake.

MESSER NICIA: Ca, ca, pu, pu. What... what... what was it made of?

LIGURIO: Aloes.

MESSER NICIA: Damn you! Spu, spu. Master, aren't you going to say something?

FRIAR TIMOTEO: Ligurio has made me angry.

MESSER NICIA: Oh, you disguise your voice very well.

LIGURIO: Let's not waste any more time here: I'll be the captain and deploy the troops for battle. Callimaco will take the right horn, I'll take the left; the doctor will hold down the middle between the two horns; Siro will be the rear-guard, to back up whatever part gives way. The password will be San Cuckoo.

MESSER NICIA: Who is San Cuckoo?

LIGURIO: He is the most honored saint in all of France. Let's go; we'll lay the ambush at this corner. Sh, listen, I hear a lute.

MESSER NICIA: That's what it is; what shall we do?

LIGURIO: We'd better send out a scout to find out who's coming, and we'll act on whatever he reports.

MESSER NICIA: Who'll go?

LIGURIO: You go, Siro, you know what to do; observe, study the situation, hurry back, report.

SIRO: I'm off. (*Leaves.*)

MESSER NICIA: I hope we don't catch a crab that turns out to be some sickly, weak old man so that we would have to play this game all over again tomorrow night.

LIGURIO: Don't worry, Siro is an expert. Here he is, he's back. What's there, Siro?

SIRO: It's the finest young rascal you ever saw. He's barely twenty-five and he's coming alone, in a ragged cloak, playing his lute.

MESSER NICIA: He's what we want, if you're telling the truth; but watch out, or this whole stew will be dumped on your head.

SIRO: He's just like I've described him.

LIGURIO: Let's wait for him to turn the corner and then we'll pounce on him.

MESSER NICIA: Come over this way, master; you act like you were made of wood. Here he comes!

CALLIMACO: (*Singing*)
> Since I can't be with you tonight in bed,
> I hope you find the devil there instead!

LIGURIO: Hold still! Hand over that lute!

CALLIMACO: Oh! What did I do?

MESSER NICIA: You'll find out. Cover his head, gag him.

LIGURIO: Spin him around.

MESSER NICIA: Give him another spin, give him another; and into the house with him. (*Poking with his sword.*)

FRIAR TIMOTEO: Messer Nicia, I'm going home to rest, for I have a terrible headache; and if you don't need me for anything else, I won't come back tomorrow morning.

MESSER NICIA: Of course, master, you don't have to come back; we can manage by ourselves. (*Follows the others into the house.*)

FRIAR TIMOTEO: They are hidden away in the house, and I'm going back to the convent; and you in the audience, don't be impatient with us, for tonight none of us is going to sleep, so that time will not interrupt the action. Ligurio and Siro will dine, for they haven't eaten all day; the doctor will pace from one room to the other to see that all goes well; Callimaco and Donna Lucrezia won't sleep, for I know that, if I were he and you were she, we wouldn't sleep.

SONG

Sweet night, O saintly, still
Nocturnal hours, that keep true
Lovers company! Such joys fill
Your every moment, that in you
Alone all souls find happiness.
With fitting gifts you bless
The swarms of lovers through their length
Of breathless labors. Hours sweet!
You, with your ever-burning strength,
Can melt the coldest hearts that beat.

ACT V

SCENE 1

Friar Timoteo.

FRIAR TIMOTEO: I haven't slept a wink all night because I've been so anxious to learn how Callimaco and the others have made out. And I busied myself with many things to kill time: I recited matins, I read a life of the holy fathers, I went into church and lit a candle that was spent, I changed the veil on a Madonna that works miracles. How many times have I told these friars to keep her neat and clean? And then they can't understand why devotions lag! I can remember when there were five hundred votive plaques and today there aren't even twenty. And the fault is ours, for not having done what we should to keep up her reputation. Every evening, after compline, we used to have a procession for her, and we used to have hymns sung in her honor every Saturday. We ourselves always used to make votive offerings there, so that there were always new plaques to be seen; and we used to encourage men and women, in confession, to make votive offerings there. Now, none of these things is done; and then we wonder why everything turns cold! Oh, how empty-headed these friars of mine are! But I hear a great commotion in Messer Nicia's house. By heaven, here they come, and they're scooting out the prisoner. I've come just in time. They certainly have lingered over the last drops; it's already getting light. I'm going to stand by and hear what they say, without showing myself.

SCENE 2

Messer Nicia, Callimaco, Ligurio, Siro.

MESSER NICIA: Grab him on that side; I'll take this side; and you, Siro, hold him by the cloak from behind.

CALLIMACO: Don't hurt me!

LIGURIO: Don't be afraid—just beat it!

MESSER NICIA: Let's not go any further.

LIGURIO: You're right—let him go here. We'll give him a couple of turns, so that he won't know where he came from. Spin him around, Siro!

SIRO: There.

MESSER NICIA: Give him another spin.

SIRO: There you are!

CALLIMACO: My lute!

LIGURIO: Beat it, you rascal—get going. If I hear you saying a word, I'll cut your throat.

MESSER NICIA: He's gone. Let's get out of these outfits; and we'd better all be up and about bright and early, so that it won't seem as if we've been up all night.

LIGURIO: That's right.

MESSER NICIA: You and Siro go to Master Callimaco and tell him that the thing went off very well.

LIGURIO: What can we tell him? We don't know anything. You know that, when we got to the house, we went right down into the wine cellar to drink. You and your mother-in-law had him in hand, and we didn't see you again until just now when you called us to put him out.

MESSER NICIA: That's right. Oh, I have some beautiful things to tell you! My wife was in bed in the dark. Sostrata was waiting for me by the fire. I came up with this young scamp and, to make sure nothing was overlooked, I led him into the pantry off the dining room where there was a weak lamp that gave off such a faint light that he couldn't see my face.

LIGURIO: Wisely done!

MESSER NICIA: I made him undress. He was whimpering. I turned on him like a dog so that it seemed a thousand years to him before he could strip off his clothes, and he stood there naked. His face is ugly. He had a monstrous nose, a twisted mouth—but you never saw such beautiful flesh! White, soft, smooth—and about the rest—don't ask me!

LIGURIO: It's better not to talk about it, for everything had to be examined.

MESSER NICIA: You're pulling my leg! Since I had stuck my hand in the dough, I wanted to touch bottom. I wanted to be sure he was healthy. Suppose he had had sores, where would I be? You tell me!

LIGURIO: You're absolutely right!

MESSER NICIA: As soon as I had made sure he was healthy, I dragged him after me and led him into the bedroom, in the dark. I put him to bed and, before leaving, I wanted to feel with my own hands how things were going, for I'm not used to being fooled into mistaking fireflies for lanterns.

LIGURIO: You did everything very sensibly.

MESSER NICIA: When I had touched and felt everything, I left the room and locked the door, and I went back to my mother-in-law who was by the fire, and we spent the whole night talking.

LIGURIO: What did you talk about?

MESSER NICIA: About Lucrezia's foolishness, and about how much better it would have been if, without so much bickering, she had given in at the very beginning. Then we talked about the baby—I feel as if I were holding him in my arms already, the chubby little fellow!—until I heard the clock strike seven, and, fearing that daylight might overtake us,

I went into the bedroom—and what do you think? I couldn't get that rascal to get up!

LIGURIO: I believe it!

MESSER NICIA: He liked the ointment! But he got up, finally; then I called you, and we put him out.

LIGURIO: The thing has gone well.

MESSER NICIA: Would you believe it, that I feel bad about it?

LIGURIO: About what?

MESSER NICIA: About that poor young fellow who will have to die so soon, and will have to pay so dearly for this night.

LIGURIO: Oh, don't give it a thought! Let him worry about it!

MESSER NICIA: You're right. But it will seem a thousand years before I can see Master Callimaco to rejoice with him.

LIGURIO: He'll be out in an hour. But it's broad daylight already; we're going to take off these clothes—what are you going to do?

MESSER NICIA: I'll go home, also, to put on my good clothes. I'll make my wife get up and wash and come to church for the blessing. I'd like you and Callimaco to be there, so that we can talk to the friar to thank him and repay him for the good he has done us.

LIGURIO: That's a good idea. We'll do it.

SCENE 3

Friar Timoteo.

FRIAR TIMOTEO: I heard that conversation and enjoyed it, just considering how stupid this doctor is. But the conclusion delighted me most of all; and since they will be coming to see me here, I'd better not stay outside any longer but wait for them in church, where my wares will have greater value. But who is coming out of that house? It looks like Ligurio, and that must be Callimaco with him. I don't want them to see me, for the reasons already given. Anyway, even if they don't come to look for me, there will be time enough for me to look for them. (*Goes into the church.*)

SCENE 4

Callimaco, Ligurio.

CALLIMACO: As I was telling you, my dear Ligurio, I had some misgivings about being there until around three in the morning; for, although it gave me great pleasure, it didn't seem quite right. But then, when I was finally able to tell her who I was and how much I loved her and how easily, because of the simple-mindedness of her husband, we could find happiness together without the slightest scandal, promising her that whenever God should will to take him away I would make her my wife; and when, on top of these good reasons, she had tasted the difference between my embrace and that of Messer Nicia, and between the kisses of a young lover and those of an old husband—after sighing a little, she said: "Since your cunning, my husband's stupidity, my mother's foolishness, and the wickedness of my confessor have led me to do what I would never have done of myself, I'm ready to believe it was heaven's will that it should all happen in this way, and I don't have it in me to reject what heaven wants me to accept. Therefore, I receive you as lord, master, guide; I want you to be my father, my protector, my every good; and what my husband has wanted for one night I want him to have always. You shall become the godfather, therefore; you shall come to church this morning and from there you will come home with him to dine with us. You'll come and go as you please, and we'll be able to meet at any time, without arousing the least suspicion." When I heard these words I was almost overcome by their sweetness. I was unable to utter the least part of what I would have liked to say. So that I'm now the happiest and most contented man who ever lived; and if this happiness could not be taken from me by death or time, I would be more blessed than the blessed, more sainted than the saints.

LIGURIO: I take great pleasure in your every good fortune; and everything turned out exactly as I said it would. But what do we do now?

CALLIMACO: Let's go toward the church, for she, her mother, and the doctor will be there, and I promised to meet them.

LIGURIO: Someone is opening their door; it's the women; they're coming out and the doctor is right behind them.

CALLIMACO: Let's go into the church, and wait there.

SCENE 5

Messer Nicia, Lucrezia, Sostrata.

MESSER NICIA: Lucrezia, I think we should do things in a God-fearing way and not foolishly.

LUCREZIA: What has to be done now?

MESSER NICIA: Listen to her, the way she answers! She looks like a rooster!

SOSTRATA: Don't be surprised, she's a little upset.

LUCREZIA: What are you trying to say?

MESSER NICIA: I say that I'd better go ahead and talk to the friar and tell him to come out to meet you in front of the church to take you in for the blessing, for it's really as if you were being born anew this morning.

LUCREZIA: Well, why don't you go?

MESSER NICIA: You're very bold this morning! Last night she looked half dead!

LUCREZIA: Thanks to you.

SOSTRATA: Go and find the friar. But never mind, there he is outside the church.

MESSER NICIA: So he is.

SCENE 6

Friar Timoteo, Messer Nicia, Lucrezia, Callimaco.

FRIAR TIMOTEO: (*To the audience*) I come out here because Callimaco and Ligurio have told me the doctor and the women are on their way to church.

MESSER NICIA: Bona dies, Father.

FRIAR TIMOTEO: Welcome! Congratulations, my lady! And, by God's grace, may you have a fine baby boy.

LUCREZIA: May it be God's will.

FRIAR TIMOTEO: It will be his will, certainly.

MESSER NICIA: Do I see Ligurio and Master Callimaco in church?

FRIAR TIMOTEO: Yes, Messere.

MESSER NICIA: Call them.

FRIAR TIMOTEO: Come here!

CALLIMACO: God keep you!

MESSER NICIA: Master, place your hand here on my wife.

CALLIMACO: Most willingly!

MESSER NICIA: Lucrezia, this is the man who shall have been the cause of our having a cane on which to prop our old age.

LUCREZIA: I hold him very dear; and I should like him to be the godfather.

MESSER NICIA: Oh, bless you! And I want him and Ligurio to come and dine with us today.

LUCREZIA: By all means!

MESSER NICIA: And I want to give them the key to the downstairs room that opens on the terrace, so that they can come whenever they like, for they have no women at home and live like beasts.

CALLIMACO: I accept it, to use when I have occasion.

FRIAR TIMOTEO: Am I to have the money for alms?

MESSER NICIA: But of course! It will be sent today, domine!

LIGURIO: Is there no one with a thought for Siro?

MESSER NICIA: Let him ask—whatever I have is his. You, Lucrezia, how many groschen are you supposed to give the friar for the blessing?

LUCREZIA: Give him ten.

MESSER NICIA: (*Choking*) Guullp!!!

FRIAR TIMOTEO: Donna Sostrata, you look as if you had a new lease on life.

SOSTRATA: Who wouldn't be gay!

FRIAR TIMOTEO: Let us all go into the church, and there we will recite the usual prayers; then, after the service, you will go to dine at your leisure. (*Pausing alone on the threshold of the church*) You people in the audience—don't wait for us to come out again; the service is long and I'll stay in the church afterward; and the others will use the side door to go home. Good-by!

SONG [1]

Because we know that life is short,
And we know what a weight of care,
Living and striving, each of us must bear,

We idle away the length of our years
Pursuing each whim without measure;
For he who denies himself pleasure,
To live a life full of anguish and tears,
Must be someone naively blind,
Ignoring how the world deceives,
And what devices fortune weaves
To overtake and to ensnare mankind.

We've chosen to flee from such sordid cares;
And, far from this sad world's confusion,
We now live in festive seclusion,
Happy youths and nymphs. With our tuneful airs
And merry rhymes, we gather in your sight,
So far from our accustomed way,
Only to keep this holiday
—And to enjoy your company tonight.

---

[1] This song, usually printed as an introduction to the *Mandragola,* and the four songs between the acts were written by Machiavelli for a special performance of the play in Modena in 1526. In the present translation the songs between the acts are printed where they usually appear in modern editions, but the "introductory" song has been removed to this place because its particular reference deprives it of relevance as a general introduction.

But the name of your ruler also draws
Us here—in whom the bright reflection
Of virtues of divine perfection
Is visible. Those virtues are the cause
Of your well-being here below.
They guarantee your worldly gains,
And they secure the peace that reigns;
So thank him from whom all your blessings flow.

The Library of Liberal Arts

Below is a representative selection from The Library of Liberal Arts. This partial listing—taken from the more than 200 scholarly editions of the world's finest literature and philosophy—indicates the scope, nature, and concept of this distinguished series.